Welcome

Words can't fully convey how much we all love Taylor Swift. The world's biggest superstar is not only a brilliant singer-songwriter, she's also a fantastic role model and an inspiration to us all to live our best lives. We all enjoy listening to her tunes, love following her cool fashions and watching her strut her stuff like no other on stage. So how better to indulge our adoration of all things Taylor than spending time being creative and proving our true fan status with a feature-packed bookazine offering colouring and other activities. Inside this special celebration of Taylor Swift, you have the chance to prove your artistic skills by colouring in 30 brilliant illustrations. You'll find each has a quote from Taylor, as well as a colourised drawing that you can use as a guide on colours – or completely ignore and go apply your own unique creative vision! We've also several quizzes and puzzles, ranging from easy to expert, to test your Tay Tay knowledge, as well as an exclusive, easy-to-enter prize competition giving you the opportunity to win THREE Taylor Swift vinyl albums!
So get colouring, solve our fun puzzles and quizzes, then be sure to enter our competition for your chance to win. Enjoy!

Contents

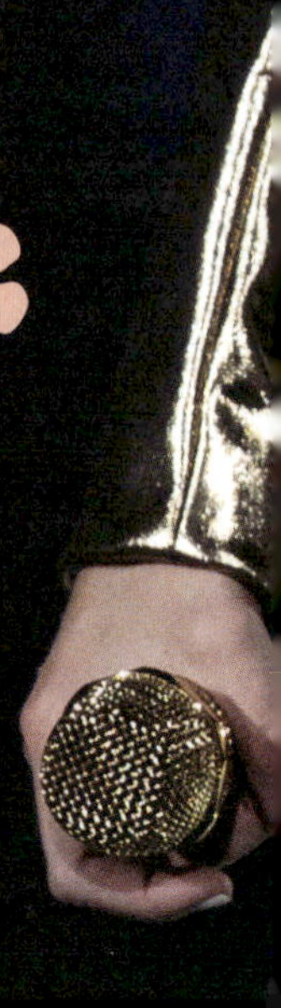

Tick off the illustrations as you complete them!

PAGE 9
PAGE 11
PAGE 13
PAGE 15
PAGE 17
PAGE 19
PAGE 21
PAGE 23
PAGE 25
PAGE 27
PAGE 29
PAGE 31
PAGE 33
PAGE 35

PAGE 37

PAGE 39

PAGE 41

PAGE 43

PAGE 45

PAGE 47

PAGE 49

PAGE 51

PAGE 53

PAGE 55

PAGE 57

PAGE 59

PAGE 61

PAGE 63

PAGE 65

PAGE 67

> "You have to believe in love stories and Prince Charmings and happily ever after"

TAYLOR SWIFT'S ERAS TOUR HAS ROCKED OUR WORLD!

GET CREATIVE WITH *YOUR* COLOURS

"*I feel like my music has become a lot of things. It's hard to label the evolution, but I like there to be an evolution*"

WE LOVE HOW COOL TAYLOR LOOKS IN THIS DRESS!

GET CREATIVE WITH *YOUR* COLOURS

"My favorite thing in life is writing about life, specifically the parts of life concerning love. Because, as far as I'm concerned, love is absolutely everything"

WE'RE SO IMPRESSED BY HOW WELL TAYLOR PLAYS THE PIANO.

GET CREATIVE WITH *YOUR* COLOURS

"Anything you put your mind to and add your imagination into can make your life a lot better and a lot more fun"

WE LOVE THIS LOOK FROM WAY BACK IN 2018!

GET CREATIVE WITH *YOUR* COLOURS

"I get so excited when a song I wrote that's very personal to me goes No. 1 and I look down and see people singing the words back to me"

WE THINK PURPLE
REALLY SUITS TAYLOR!

GET CREATIVE WITH *YOUR* COLOURS

> "FASHION IS ALL ABOUT PLAYFUL EXPERIMENTATION. IF YOU DON'T LOOK BACK AT PICTURES OF SOME OF YOUR OLD LOOKS AND CRINGE, YOU'RE DOING IT WRONG"

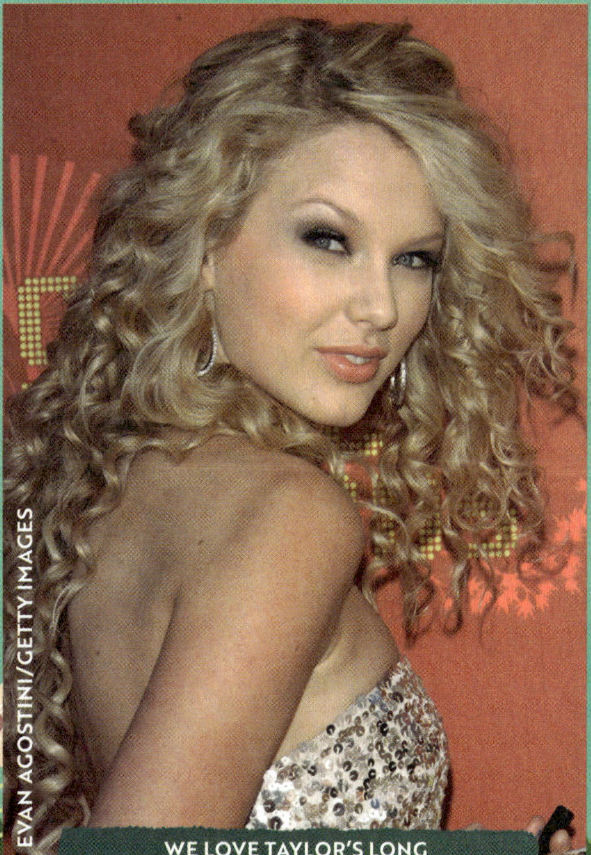

WE LOVE TAYLOR'S LONG CURLY HAIR FROM HER YOUNGER YEARS!

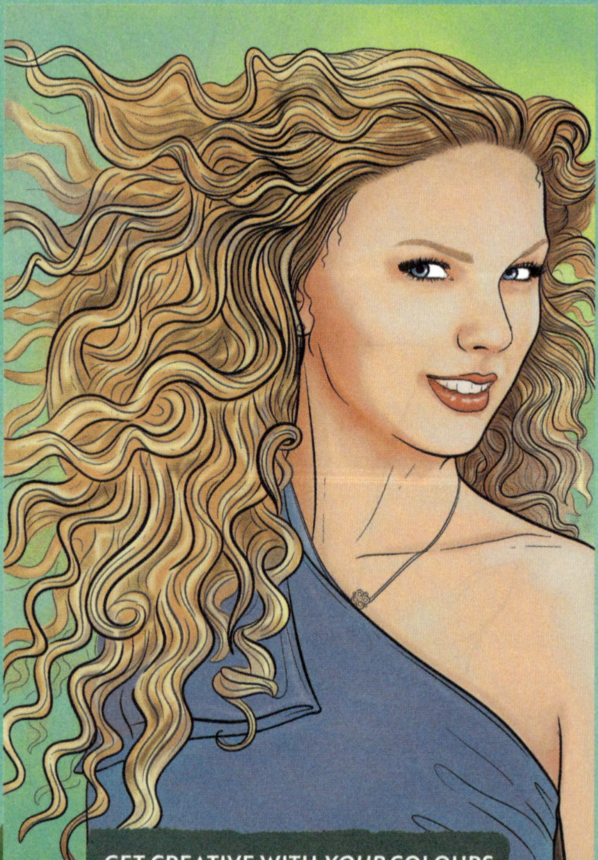

GET CREATIVE WITH *YOUR* COLOURS

> *"I write songs to help me understand life a little more. I write songs to get past things that cause me pain"*

NOTHING BEATS THE ERAS TOUR BODYSUIT LOOK!

GET CREATIVE WITH *YOUR* COLOURS

JORDAN STRAUSS/INVISION/AP

TAYLOR LOOKS AMAZING AT THE 66TH GRAMMY AWARDS IN 2024.

GET CREATIVE WITH *YOUR* COLOURS

"YOU HAVE TO PRACTICE TO BE GOOD AT GUITAR. YOU HAVE TO WRITE 100 SONGS BEFORE YOU WRITE THE FIRST GOOD ONE"

TAYLOR LOOKS AMAZING WHEN PLAYING THE GUITAR!

GET CREATIVE WITH *YOUR* COLOURS

WE ADORE THE BEAUTY OF TAYLOR'S FOLKLORE OUTFITS.

GET CREATIVE WITH *YOUR* COLOURS

CHECK OUT THOSE LOUBOUTIN BOOTS!

GET CREATIVE WITH *YOUR* COLOURS

"I didn't want to just be another girl singer. I wanted there to be something that set me apart"

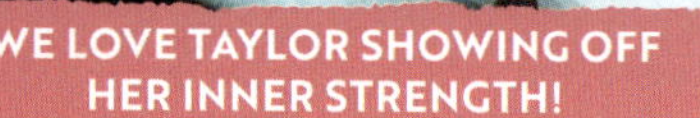

WE LOVE TAYLOR SHOWING OFF HER INNER STRENGTH!

GET CREATIVE WITH *YOUR* COLOURS

WENN RIGHTS LTD / ALAMY STOCK PHOTO

TAYLOR WEARS BLACK AND WHITE ON HER *RED* TOUR SET.

GET CREATIVE WITH *YOUR* COLOURS

> "I don't live by all these rigid, weird rules that make me feel all fenced in. I just like the way that I feel like, and that makes me feel very free"

TAYLOR DAZZLES IN ONE OF HER *FOLKLORE* GOWNS.

GET CREATIVE WITH *YOUR* COLOURS

WE LOVE THE ICONIC SUNGLASSES LOOK FROM TAYLOR'S *1989* TOUR.

GET CREATIVE WITH *YOUR* COLOURS

"THEY CAN SAY WHATEVER THEY WANT ABOUT MY PERSONAL LIFE BECAUSE I KNOW WHAT MY PERSONAL LIFE IS, AND IT INVOLVES A LOT OF TV AND CATS AND GIRLFRIENDS"

WE LOVE THE FACT THAT TAYLOR'S A CATWOMAN!

GET CREATIVE WITH *YOUR* COLOURS

> *"I like touring extensively because I think the more hours you spend onstage, the more you know who you are onstage"*

WE LOVE HOW TAYLOR ENJOYS PLEASING HER FANS!

GET CREATIVE WITH *YOUR* COLOURS

"All my mornings are Mondays stuck in an endless February"

TAYLOR LOOKS SO DREAMY IN ONE OF HER NEWEST DRESSES.

GET CREATIVE WITH *YOUR* COLOURS

NOTHING BEATS SEEING TAYLOR LOOK SO HAPPY ON STAGE!

GET CREATIVE WITH *YOUR* COLOURS

"I don't compare myself to anyone else; I don't make comments about anyone else because they do what feels right for them, and that's okay by me"

IMAGE PRESS AGENCY / ALAMY STOCK PHOTO

TAYLOR'S A WINNER IN HER GREEN GOWN AT THE GOLDEN GLOBES!

GET CREATIVE WITH *YOUR* COLOURS

> ## "I have this really high priority on happiness and finding something to be happy about"

OUR FAVOURITE FOLKLORE OUTFIT BY FAR!

GET CREATIVE WITH *YOUR* COLOURS

TAYLOR POINTS TO HER THOUSANDS OF FANS – INCLUDING US!

KATE GREEN/GETTY IMAGES

GET CREATIVE WITH *YOUR* COLOURS

Which Taylor Swift music video is the inspiration for our illustration?

ANSWER: SHAKE IT OFF

WE LOVE TAYLOR SWIFT AND SHE LOVES US BACK!

GET CREATIVE WITH *YOUR* COLOURS

Which Taylor Swift music video is the inspiration for our illustration?

ANSWER: 22

GET CREATIVE WITH *YOUR* COLOURS

NOT
A LOT
GOING ON
TH
MOMENT

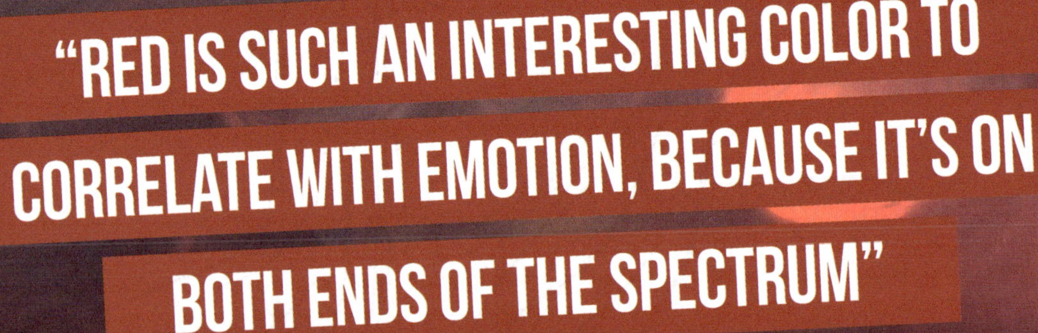

Which Taylor Swift music video is the inspiration for our illustration?

ANSWER: I BET YOU THINK ABOUT ME (TAYLOR'S VERSION)

"*Silence speaks so much louder than screaming tantrums. Never give anyone an excuse to say that you're crazy.*"

TAYLOR ALWAYS INSPIRES US WITH HER AMAZING PERFORMANCES AND OUTFITS.

GET CREATIVE WITH *YOUR* COLOURS

"I have been singing randomly, obsessively, obnoxiously for as long as I can remember"

YOU CAN'T HELP BUT SING ALONG TO ALL THE HITS FROM *MIDNIGHTS*!

GET CREATIVE WITH *YOUR* COLOURS

TAYLOR ALWAYS INSPIRES US TO BE THE BEST WE CAN!

GET CREATIVE WITH *YOUR* COLOURS

> ## "We could leave the Christmas lights up 'til January... this is our place, we make the rules"

ONLY SEEING SANTA COULD TOP SEEING TAYLOR AT CHRISTMAS!

KAMIL KRZACZYNSKI/AFP VIA GETTY IMAGES

GET CREATIVE WITH *YOUR* COLOURS

Activities & Quizzes

Test your Taylor Swift knowledge on our puzzle-filled pages
Tick them off once you've finished them!

Word Searches

Puzzles

Quizzes

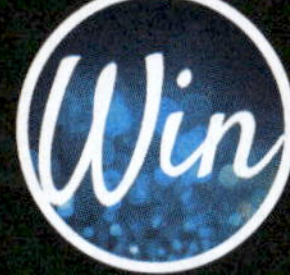

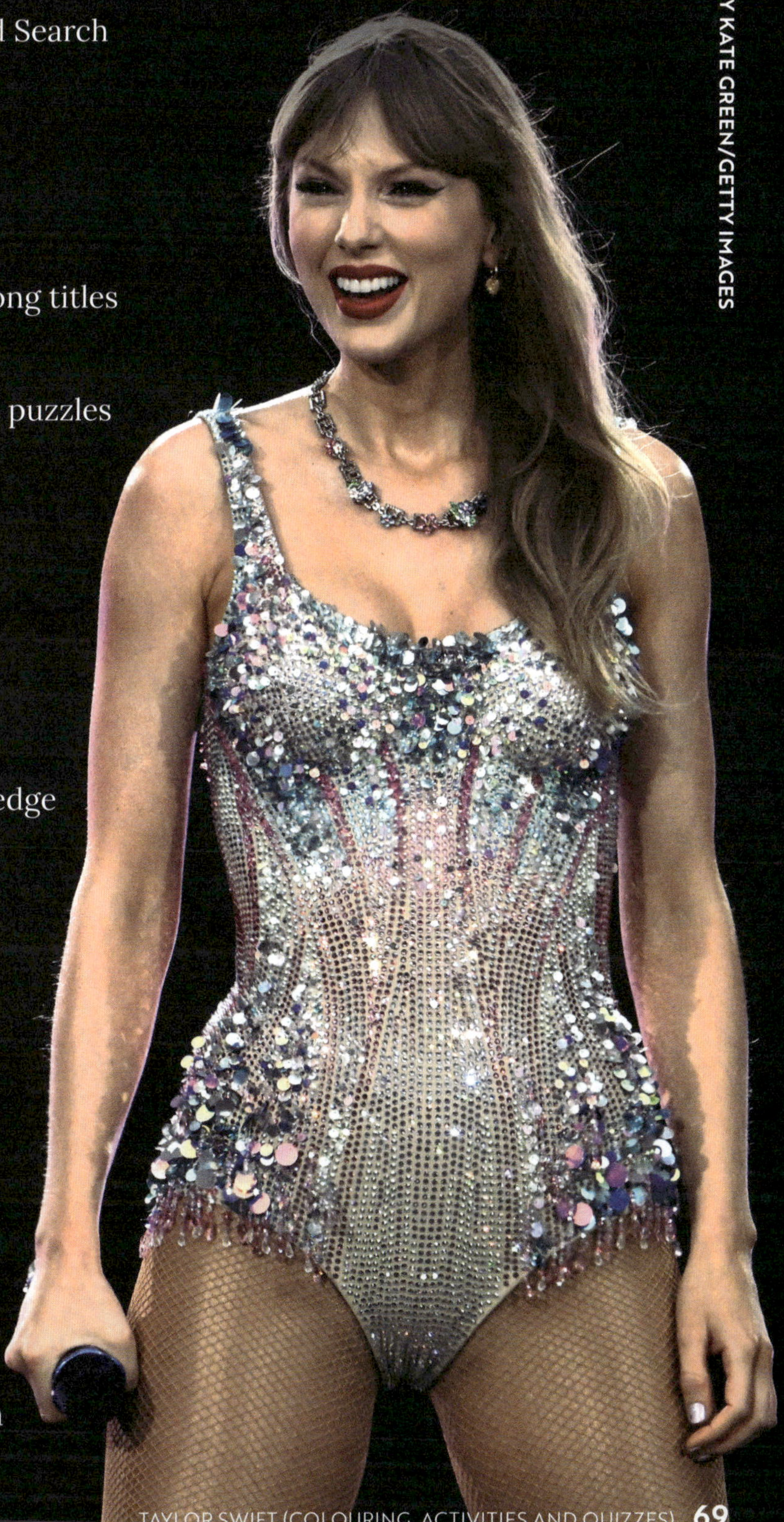

PHOTO BY KATE GREEN/GETTY IMAGES

Win

Prize Competition

Taylor's Musical Word Search

We've hidden several Taylor-themed musical words in this puzzle – can you find them?

```
E Y B S O S T K C F K L J T A
G S Z N L R K G Z Q B B R M A
R D S C U E J M A R J O R I E
S S W A J D F E A R L E S S Z
Z J K G U I T A R V T Y K Z B
L F A M E G R A M M Y S Z U I
O O R I J Z G Q F L A P S I E
V L M D G D S J P X U U J Y Z
E K A N N A S H V I L L E M Y
R L X I N V K Q T K G L K Q
S O Y G Z E R A P L U K S E Z
A R X H J G H P Z P F C T R S
N E Z T T R Y A R M U N L A C
U P D S B E J E W E L E D S P
Z O M C X C Y X Z P L I M Z K
```

Try to find all 12 words:

Midnights	Bejeweled	Red
Fearless	Eras	Grammys
Guitar	Folklore	Karma
Nashville	Marjorie	Lover

Taylor's Friends & Family Word Search

Can you find the names of important people in Taylor's life in this puzzle?

```
G P O U B N X Y Z X R C O A Y
X D C S T O D R I C K X M J O
S O I E N G Y L L E N H A A L
E C A U S T I N Q C A L V I N
L H Q R L C T R A V I S G M X
E H B U O B B S T B K U C X N
N O A X F N E H S D Y S E K H
A P I I K P Q E A B I G A I L
T V W P M G G E Q J G Z Z A H
K Y B J Z B J R L L S P R G S
W S O Z L I Y A W B E C Q I P
C D L P J R T N C Y J S O R W
J U Q D O J G A N D R E A T D
R R Q I E S H D E S S N E R T
Q K H I A N T O N O F F I N N
```

Try to find all 14 words:

Gyllenhaal   Joe   Todrick   Scott

Antonoff   Abigail   Travis   Haim

Dessner   Sheeran   Austin   Selena

Andrea   Calvin

ASHOK KUMAR/TAS24/GETTY IMAGES

Taylor's Lyrics Word Search

Can you find our selection of lyrics from Taylor's songs in this puzzle?

```
I Q M A X Y M W S Z H K K D S
B A C R Y S T A L X G E R M C
F T O C A R D I G A N M A G Z
J O N O I L L I C I T A I D B
H P A T R I A R C H Y C N R R
K O A H Y G H O S T S H H E F
H O R N L U O U D O D I V A N
F T C K F F G V S A A A P M P
Y T H P A E A U H L Z V O D I
P J E I N V I S I B L E L Q M
G P R V J E D K G Q B L A U G
S F A U M R P A X Y P L R O M
I I D F C A M B E R W I O S N
E D E T C R I N I T C A I J O
R M A S Q U E R A D E N D I T
```

Try to find all 14 words:

Machiavellian	Illicit	Rain	Dream
Patriarchy	Invisible	Archer	Amber
Masquerade	Cardigan	Crystal	Fever
	Polaroid	Ghosts	

Swiftie Specials Word Search

Can you find all the words that Swifties relate to Taylor in this puzzle?

```
R S M V L V T Q O T G B S P O
N X P A Y S H M F V I Z G I L
A Z H U K E I A D A A C A R H
J H C L Q L R B F T I T Y N C
E R C T O F T R U T F T I T M
C A C S S I E A O R Z A T O Y
L O S N C E E C Y C A Y H I N
E S H T R S N E F O A L A N Q
J H T T E P K L F W Y U N S A
A I J A A R U E M G O R G T X
B M X Y M L E T K I H K O A D
F M Y T N X H G N R K I U G I
J E S A K F H U G L Y N T R J
D R I Y V U L D Q S S G S A V
W T J G L I T T E R R H F M F
```

Try to find all 14 words:

Easter eggs   Cowgirls   Ovation   Selfies

Instagram   Thirteen   Tay Tay   Scream

Bracelet   Glitter   Taylurking   Vault

Shimmer   Hangouts

Find The Hidden Songs

Can you solve the anagrams and find the Taylor tracks?

01 Ah! Kites Off

02 Mr Mule Cures

03 Back Panels

04 Mealymouthed Oak Wood

05 Hair-tone

06 Ann Etched

07 Admits Welders

08 Flag Tower

09 Cobra Law

10 Admiring Hint

Answers on page 82

Cryptic Countries

Guess the names of 10 of the countries on the Eras Tour from these cryptograms.

Substitute the letters shown with alternatives to form the names of the countries. We have given you a start by revealing the letter **O is actually an A** and the letter **G is actually an S**.

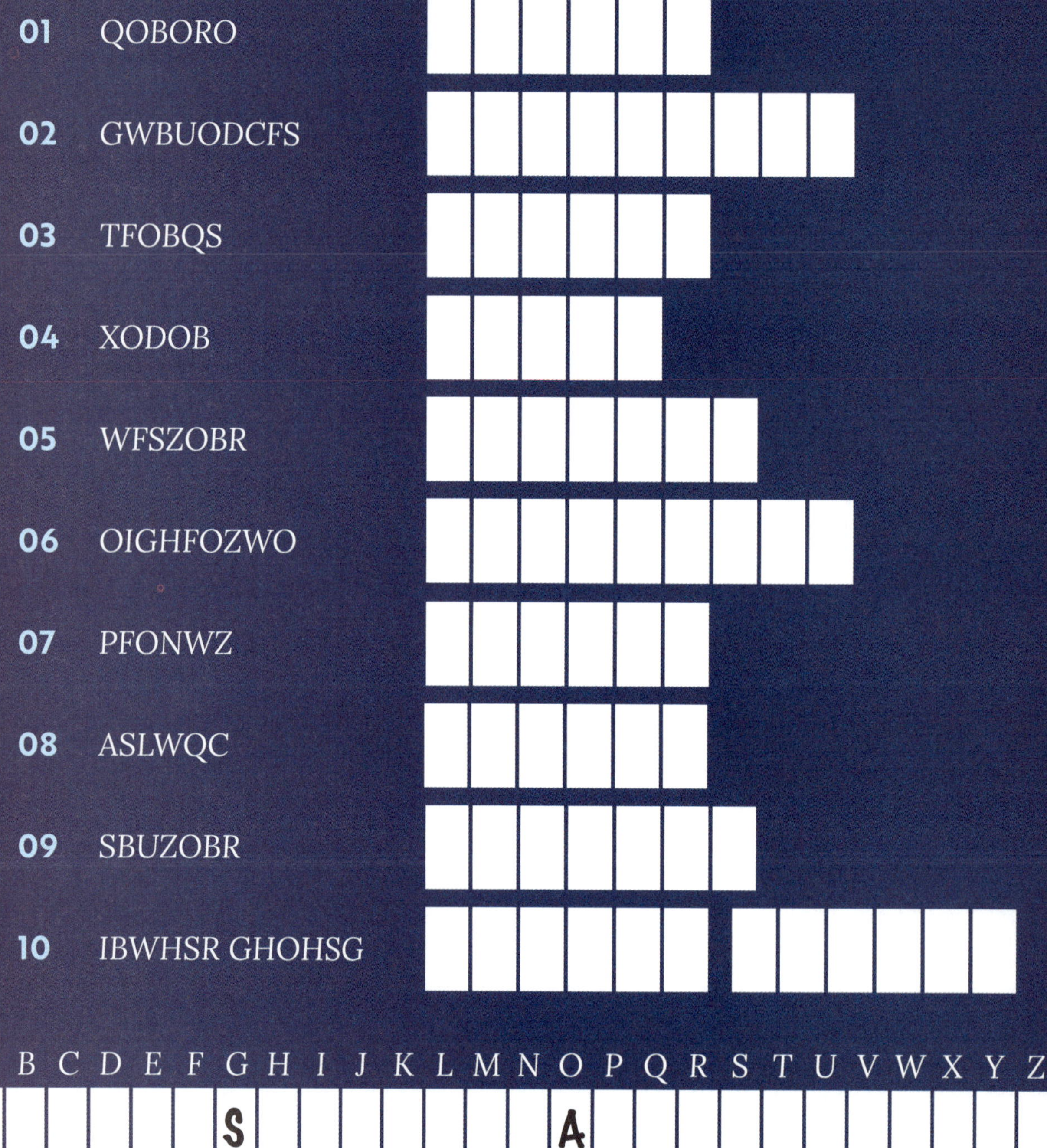

01 QOBORO

02 GWBUODCFS

03 TFOBQS

04 XODOB

05 WFSZOBR

06 OIGHFOZWO

07 PFONWZ

08 ASLWQC

09 SBUZOBR

10 IBWHSR GHOHSG

Answers on page 82

Puzzle Answers

Taylor's Musical Word Search

E	Y	B	S	O	S	T	K	C	F	K	L	J	T	A
G	S	Z	N	L	R	K	G	Z	Q	B	B	R	M	A
R	D	S	C	U	E	J	M	A	R	J	O	R	I	E
S	S	W	A	J	D	F	E	A	R	L	E	S	S	Z
Z	J	K	G	U	I	T	A	R	V	T	Y	K	Z	B
L	F	A	M	E	G	R	A	M	M	Y	S	Z	U	I
O	O	R	I	J	Z	G	Q	F	L	A	P	S	I	E
V	L	M	D	G	D	S	J	P	X	U	U	J	Y	Z
E	K	A	N	N	A	S	H	V	I	L	L	E	M	Y
R	L	X	I	X	N	V	K	Q	T	K	G	L	K	Q
S	O	Y	G	Z	E	R	A	P	L	U	K	S	E	Z
A	R	X	H	J	G	H	P	Z	P	F	C	T	R	S
N	E	Z	T	T	R	Y	A	R	M	U	N	L	A	C
U	P	D	S	B	E	J	E	W	E	L	E	D	S	P
Z	O	M	C	X	C	Y	X	Z	P	L	I	M	Z	K

Taylor's Friends & Family Word Search

G	P	O	U	B	N	X	Y	Z	X	R	C	O	A	Y
X	D	C	S	T	O	D	R	I	C	K	X	M	J	O
S	O	I	E	N	G	Y	L	L	E	N	H	A	A	L
E	C	A	U	S	T	I	N	Q	C	A	L	V	I	N
L	H	Q	R	L	C	T	R	A	V	I	S	G	M	X
E	H	B	U	O	B	B	S	T	B	K	U	C	X	N
N	O	A	X	F	N	E	H	S	D	Y	S	E	K	H
A	P	I	I	K	P	Q	E	A	B	I	G	A	I	L
T	V	W	P	M	G	G	E	Q	J	G	Z	Z	A	H
K	Y	B	J	Z	B	J	R	L	L	S	P	R	G	S
W	S	O	Z	L	I	Y	A	W	B	E	C	Q	I	P
C	D	L	P	J	R	T	N	C	Y	J	S	O	R	W
J	U	Q	D	O	J	G	A	N	D	R	E	A	T	D
R	R	Q	I	E	S	H	D	E	S	S	N	E	R	T
Q	K	H	I	A	N	T	O	N	O	F	F	I	N	N

Taylor's Lyrics Word Search

I	Q	M	A	X	Y	M	W	S	Z	H	K	K	D	S
B	A	C	R	Y	S	T	A	L	X	G	E	R	M	C
F	T	O	C	A	R	D	I	G	A	N	M	A	G	Z
J	O	N	O	I	L	L	I	C	I	T	A	I	D	B
H	P	A	T	R	I	A	R	C	H	Y	C	N	R	R
K	O	A	H	Y	G	H	O	S	T	S	H	H	E	F
H	O	R	N	L	U	O	U	D	O	D	I	V	A	N
F	T	C	K	F	F	G	V	S	A	A	A	P	M	P
Y	T	H	P	A	E	A	U	H	L	Z	V	O	D	I
P	J	E	I	N	V	I	S	I	B	L	E	L	Q	M
G	P	R	V	J	E	D	K	G	Q	B	L	A	U	G
S	F	A	U	M	R	P	A	X	Y	P	L	R	O	M
I	I	D	F	C	A	M	B	E	R	W	I	O	S	N
E	D	E	T	C	R	I	N	I	T	C	A	I	J	O
R	M	A	S	Q	U	E	R	A	D	E	N	D	I	T

Swiftie Specials Word Search

R	S	M	V	L	V	T	Q	O	T	G	B	S	P	O
N	X	P	A	Y	S	H	M	F	V	I	Z	G	I	L
A	Z	H	U	K	E	I	A	D	A	A	C	A	R	H
J	H	C	L	Q	L	R	B	F	T	I	T	Y	N	C
E	R	C	T	O	F	T	R	U	T	F	T	I	T	M
C	A	C	S	S	I	E	A	O	R	Z	A	T	O	Y
L	O	S	N	C	E	E	C	Y	C	A	Y	H	I	N
E	S	H	T	R	S	N	E	F	O	A	L	A	N	Q
J	H	T	T	E	P	K	L	F	W	Y	U	N	S	A
A	I	J	A	A	R	U	E	M	G	O	R	G	T	X
B	M	X	Y	M	L	E	T	K	I	H	K	O	A	D
F	M	Y	T	N	X	H	G	N	R	K	I	U	G	I
J	E	S	A	K	F	H	U	G	L	Y	N	T	R	J
D	R	I	Y	V	U	L	D	Q	S	S	G	S	A	V
W	T	J	G	L	I	T	T	E	R	R	H	F	M	F

Answers to Find The Hidden Songs

01 Shake It Off!
02 Cruel Summer
03 Blank Space
04 Look What You Made Me Do
05 Anti-hero
06 Enchanted
07 Wildest Dreams
08 Afterglow
09 Clara Bow
10 Midnight Rain

Answers to Cryptic Countries

01 Canada
02 Singapore
03 France
04 Japan
05 Ireland
06 Australia
07 Brazil
08 Mexico
09 England
10 United States

Twelve Questions
That Should Come Easy

01 How long was Taylor dating Joe Alwyn?

02 Who called Taylor a "snake"?

03 How long is Taylor's Version of the track *All Too Well*?

04 When did the Eras Tour begin?

05 Which albums did Taylor write during the Covid-19 pandemic?

06 Which football team does Travis Kelce play for?

07 Which of Taylor's cats is named after a character in *Grey's Anatomy*?

08 What is Taylor's brother's name?

09 Where did Taylor's career begin?

10 On which album is the song *We Are Never Ever Getting Back Together*?

11 Where is Taylor's holiday home where she holds 4th of July parties?

12 Which Taylor song begins: "We were both young when I first saw you"?

Answers on page 96

Twelve Questions
For True Taylor Fans

01 What is Taylor's middle name?

02 What year was Taylor's first album *Taylor Swift* released?

03 What is the name of the documentary Taylor made in 2020 about her life?

04 Which movie was Taylor shooting when she met Taylor Lautner?

05 Which singer should have won Best Female Video instead of Taylor at the 2009 MTV Video Music Awards, according to Kanye West?

06 How many countries did the Eras Tour visit?

07 Which four albums have been released as Taylor's Versions?

08 With which band does Taylor's songwriting collaborator Aaron Dessner play?

09 In which district of New York does Taylor have an apartment?

10 Which US rapper featured on the track *Karma*?

11 Which item of make-up gives Taylor's her signature look?

12 What do Swifties call it when Taylor comments on their social media posts?

Answers on page 96

Twelve Questions to Really Test Your Taylor Knowledge

01 Who bought Big Machine Records and Taylor's Masters from Scott Borchetta?

02 Where was Taylor born?

03 Where was the family's summer home for many years when Taylor was growing up?

04 Who was the country music composer who taught Taylor her songwriting?

05 Which *Fearless* track was written about Taylor's childhood friend Abigail?

06 Who was Taylor's personal trainer for the Eras Tour?

07 Where was Taylor singing when she was first spotted by Scott Borchetta?

08 What character did Taylor play in the movie *Cats*?

09 How does Taylor categorise the three types of lyrics she writes?

10 What are the first names of the three Haim sisters who perform with Taylor?

11 Which of Taylor's cats appeared draped round her neck on the cover of *Time* magazine in 2023?

12 Which official video features Taylor as Cinderella and the Haims as the Ugly Sisters?

Answers on page 96

SORTIE SORTIE

Fill In The Blanks

How well do you know Taylor's lyrics? Can you fill in the missing words from 10 of her greatest hits?

01 It's me, hi, I'm the problem, it's me

At _ _ _ _ _ _ _, everybody agrees

02 I'm in my room, it's a typical _ _ _ _ _ _ _ night

03 I'm listening to the kind of music she doesn't like

And I, left my _ _ _ _ _ there at your sister's house

And you've still got it in your drawer even now

04 I've got a list of names and yours is in red, _ _ _ _ _ _ _ _ _ _ _

check it once, then check it twice, oh

05 Oh, my God, look at that face

You look like my _ _ _ _ _ _ _ _ _ _ _

06 Romeo take me somewhere we can _ _ _ _ _ _ _ _

07 It's like I got this _ _ _ _ _ in my mind

Sayin' it's gonna be alright

08 There goes the maddest woman the town has ever seen

She had a marvellous time _ _ _ _ _ _ _ _ _ _ _ _ _ _ _ _ _ _

09 I broke his heart 'cause he was nice

He was _ _ _ _ _ _ _ _ _, I was midnight rain

10 I'm sick of running as fast as I can

Wonderin' if I'd get there quicker if I was _ _ _ _

Answers on page 96

Guess The Song

Which songs contain these lyrics?

01   Too high a horse/ For a simple girl/ To rise above it

02   It's cool, that's what I tell 'em/ No rules in breakable heaven

03   But if I just showed up at your party/ Would you have me? Would you want me?

04   You grew your hair long/ You got new icons

05   Your Midas touch on the Chevy door/ November flush and your flannel cure

06   Why'd you have to lead me on?/ Why'd you have to twist the knife?

07   The dopamine races through his brain/ On a six-lane Texas highway

08   Can I go where you go? Can we always be this close?

09   Watch you breathe in, watch you breathing out, out

10   You don't know about me/ But I'll bet you want to

Answers on page 96

JOHN SHEARER/TAS24/GETTY IMAGES

First Liners

Can you sing (and write in) the first line of these songs?

01   *So High School*

02   *We Are Never Ever Getting Back Together*

03   *willow*

04   *invisible string*

05   *Fortnight*

06   *...Ready For It?*

07   *You Need To Calm Down*

08   *Snow On The Beach*

09   *The Archer*

10   *Miss Americana & The Heartbreak Prince*

Answers on page 96

I BET
YOU
THINK
ABOUT
ME

Quiz Answers

Twelve Questions That Should Come Easy

01 Six years
02 Kim Kardashian
03 Ten minutes
04 March 2023
05 *folklore* and *evermore*
06 Kansas City Chiefs
07 Dr Meredith Grey
08 Austin
09 Nashville, Tennessee
10 *Red*
11 Rhode Island
12 *Love Story*

Twelve Questions For True Taylor Fans

01 Alison
02 2006
03 *Miss Americana*
04 *Valentine's Day*
05 Beyonce
06 22
07 *Fearless, Red, Speak Now* and *1989*
08 The National
09 Tribeca
10 Ice Spice
11 Red lipstick
12 Taylurking

Twelve Questions to Really Test Your Taylor Knowledge

01 Scooter Braun
02 West Reading, Pennsylvania
03 Stone Harbour, New Jersey
04 Liz Rose
05 *Fifteen*
06 Kirk Myers, who runs gyms in New York and Los Angeles
07 The Bluebird Café in Nashville
08 Bombalurina
09 Quill lyrics, Fountain Pen lyrics and Glitter Gel Pen lyrics
10 Este, Danielle and Alana
11 Benjamin Button
12 *Bejeweled*

Fill In The Blanks

01 Tea time (*Anti-Hero*)
02 Tuesday (*You Belong With Me*)
03 Scarf (*All Too Well*)
04 Underlined (*Look What You Made Me Do*)
05 Next mistake (*Blank Space*)
06 Be Alone (*Love Story*)
07 Music (*Shake It Off*)
08 Ruining everything (*the last great american dynasty*)
09 Sunshine (*Midnight Rain*)
10 A man (*The Man*)

Guess The Song

01 *But Daddy I Love Him*
02 *Cruel Summer*
03 *betty*
04 *Now That We Don't Talk*
05 *champagne problems*
06 *Say Don't Go*
07 *I Can Fix Him (No I Really Can)*
08 *Lover*
09 *epiphany*
10 *22*

First Liners

01 I feel so high school every time I look at you/ I wanna find you in a crowd just to hide from you

02 I remember when we broke up the first time/ Saying, "This is it, I've had enough," 'cause like/ We hadn't seen each other in a month

03 I'm like the water when your ship rolled in that night/ Rough on the surface but you cut through like a knife

04 Green was the color of the grass/ Where I used to read at Centennial Park

05 I was supposed to be sent away/ But they forgot to come and get me

06 Knew he was a killer first time that I saw him/ Wonder how many girls he had loved and left haunted

07 You are somebody that I don't know/ But you're taking shots at me like it's Patrón

08 One night, a few moons ago/ I saw flecks of what could've been lights

09 Combat, I'm ready for combat/ I say I don't want that, but what if I do?

10 You know I adore you, I'm crazier for you/ Than I was at 16, lost in a film scene

Your chance to own THREE Taylor Swift albums on vinyl!

Now that you've coloured in lots of Taylor Swift illustrations and proved what an amazing fan you are by completing our puzzles and quizzes, it's time to take part in our easy to enter competition. We're giving you the chance to win a prize bundle made up of three Taylor Swift albums on vinyl as follows:

- *Red* (Taylor's Version) triple LP
- *1989* (Taylor's Version) double LP set - Crystal Skies Blue edition
- *Evermore* double LP set - green vinyl edition

Winning this amazing prize couldn't be easier – all you have to do is scan the QR code with your smartphone (or type the url into your web browser), fill in your details, and that's it – you're in with a chance of winning this amazing prize! Closing date for entries is April 30, 2025.

This competition is restricted to entrants aged 18 years or over. If you're under 18, a parent or guardian must enter on your behalf giving their full details. Only one entry per person is permitted. Full terms and conditions can be found at: **https://shop.keypublishing.com/pages/win3taylorswift**

Scan with your phone to enter

If you can't use our QR code don't worry, you can still enter by typing the following into your web browser:

https://shop.keypublishing.com/pages/win3taylorswift